People in My Community

Crossing Guard

by JoAnn Early Macken
Photographs by Gregg Andersen

Reading consultant: Susan Nations, M.Ed., author/literacy coach/consultant

WEEKLY WR READER®
EARLY LEARNING LIBRARY

Please visit our web site at: www.earlyliteracy.cc
For a free color catalog describing Weekly Reader® Early Learning Library's
list of high-quality books, call 1-877-445-5824 (USA) or 1-800-387-3178 (Canada).
Weekly Reader® Early Learning Library's fax: (414) 336-0164.

Library of Congress Cataloging-in-Publication Data

Macken, JoAnn Early, 1953-
    Crossing guard / by JoAnn Early Macken.
        p. cm. — (People in my community)
    Summary: Photographs and simple text describe the work done by school crossing guards.
    Includes bibliographical references and index.
    ISBN 0-8368-3589-1 (lib. bdg.)
    ISBN 0-8368-3596-4 (softcover)
    1. School crossing guards—Juvenile literature. [1. School crossing guards.] I. Title.
II. Series.
LB2865.M33   2003
363.12'57—dc21
                                      2002038026

First published in 2003 by
Weekly Reader® Early Learning Library
330 West Olive Street, Suite 100
Milwaukee, WI 53212 USA

Art direction: Tammy Gruenewald
Page layout: Katherine A. Goedheer
Photographer: Gregg Andersen
Editorial assistant: Diane Laska-Swanke

Printed in the United States of America

1 2 3 4 5 6 7 8 9 07 06 05 04 03

Note to Educators and Parents

Reading is such an exciting adventure for young children! They are beginning to integrate their oral language skills with written language. To encourage children along the path to early literacy, books must be colorful, engaging, and interesting; they should invite the young reader to explore both the print and the pictures.

People in My Community is a new series designed to help children read about the world around them. In each book young readers will learn interesting facts about some familiar community helpers.

Each book is specially designed to support the young reader in the reading process. The familiar topics are appealing to young children and invite them to read — and re-read — again and again. The full-color photographs and enhanced text further support the student during the reading process.

In addition to serving as wonderful picture books in schools, libraries, homes, and other places where children learn to love reading, these books are specifically intended to be read within an instructional guided reading group. This small group setting allows beginning readers to work with a fluent adult model as they make meaning from the text. After children develop fluency with the text and content, the book can be read independently. Children and adults alike will find these books supportive, engaging, and fun!

— Susan Nations, M.Ed., author, literacy coach,
and consultant in literacy development

A crossing guard
helps children walk
to school safely.
He stops traffic
so children can
cross the street.

Children wait on the sidewalk until the crossing guard tells them to walk.

A crossing guard holds a **flag** or a stop sign. Flags and stop signs tell drivers to stop.

flag

Cars, trucks, and buses stop and wait. Then the school crossing guard tells children it is safe to cross the street.

Sometimes, the crossing guard walks with the children to make sure they cross safely.

13

A crossing guard wears a bright **vest**, sash, or raincoat. Drivers can see the bright colors.

vest

Crossing guards must learn safety rules. They must know how to signal traffic to stop and go.

Do you know how to cross a street safely? Always cross at a corner. Wait on the **curb**, and look both ways for cars.

curb

Never run into a street or an alley. Listen to your school crossing guard. Be safe!

Glossary

sash — a band worn over one shoulder or around the waist

signal — make a movement that sends a message

traffic — cars, trucks, buses, and other things moving on the street

vest — a short, sleeveless jacket

For More Information

Fiction Books

Rathman, Peggy. *Officer Buckle and Gloria.*
New York: G. P. Putnam's Sons, 1995.
Rockwell, Anne F. *Career Day.* New York:
HarperCollins Publishers, 2000.

Nonfiction Books

DeGezelle, Terri. *School Crossing Guards.*
Mankato, Minn.: Bridgestone Books, 2002.
Loewen, Nancy. *Traffic Safety.* Chanhassen,
Minn.: The Child's World, 1996.

Web Sites
Safety Tips for Walkers
www.nhtsa.dot.gov/kids/biketour/pedsafety/index.html
Department of Transportation page about pedestrian
safety

Index

alley, 20
buses, 10
cars, 10, 18
corner, 18
curb, 18
drivers, 14
flag, 8
raincoat, 14

safety rules, 16
sash, 14
sidewalk, 6
stop sign, 8
street, 4, 10, 18
traffic, 4, 16
trucks, 10
vest, 14

About the Author

JoAnn Early Macken is the author of children's poetry, two rhyming picture books, *Cats on Judy* and *Sing-Along Song,* and various other nonfiction series. She teaches children to write poetry and received the Barbara Juster Esbensen 2000 Poetry Teaching Award. JoAnn is a graduate of the MFA in Writing for Children Program at Vermont College. She lives in Wisconsin with her husband and their two sons.